The R

David Hare is the author of thirty-two full-length plays for the stage, seventeen of which have been presented at the National Theatre. They include *Slag*, *The Great Exhibition*, *Brassneck* (with Howard Brenton), *Knuckle*, *Fanshen*, *Teeth 'n' Smiles*, *Plenty*, *A Map of the World*, *Pravda* (with Howard Brenton), *The Bay at Nice*, *The Secret Rapture*, *Racing Demon*, *Murmuring Judges*, *The Absence of War*, *Skylight*, *Amy's View*, *The Blue Room* (from Schnitzler), *The Judas Kiss*, *Via Dolorosa*, *My Zinc Bed*, *The Breath of Life*, *The Permanent Way*, *Stuff Happens*, *The Vertical Hour*, *Gethsemane*, *Berlin/ Wall*, *The Power of Yes*, *South Downs* and *Behind the Beautiful Forevers*. His many screenplays for film and television include *Licking Hitler*, *Wetherby*, *Damage*, *The Hours*, *The Reader*, *Page Eight*, *Turks & Caicos* and *Salting the Battlefield*. He has also written English adaptations of plays by Brecht, Gorky, Chekhov, Pirandello, Ibsen and Lorca.

Georges Simenon was born in Liège, Belgium, in 1903. He lived in France from 1922 until the end of the Second World War, then spent ten years in the United States, before settling in Lausanne, Switzerland, where he died in 1989. Of his prolific output of over four hundred novels and short stories, he is best known as author of the Maigret detective novels. *La Main*, on which *The Red Barn* is based, was originally published in 1968.

DAVID HARE

The Red Barn

Based on *La Main*
by Georges Simenon

FABER & FABER

This edition first published in 2016
by Faber and Faber Limited
74–77 Great Russell Street
London WC1B 3DA

Typeset by Country Setting, Kingsdown, Kent CT14 8ES
Printed and bound in the UK by CPI Group (UK) Ltd, Croydon CR0 4YY

A CIP record for this book
is available from the British Library

ISBN 978-0-571-33592-3

2 4 6 8 10 9 7 5 3 1

For Bill

Introduction

Like many bookish children, I grew up consuming more detective fiction more than any other kind. Even then I had noticed that stories supposedly driven by narrative depended for their real vitality on establishing ambience. Crime writing came to life when it had density, when you felt that the paint was being laid on thick. A strong sense of time and place was far more exciting than a clever puzzle. Anyone could create a mystery, but only the best could summon up a world in which the mystery could take root.

My taste in literary fiction – I read every word of Patrick Hamilton and Graham Greene – was towards those authors whose techniques most closely resembled those of thriller writers. When, at university, I came across W. H. Auden's suggestion that Raymond Chandler's books 'should be read and judged, not as escape literature, but as works of art' I was bewildered. It had never occurred to me that thrillers were anything less. By then I had already graduated from Agatha Christie and Dorothy Sayers to Dashiell Hammett and the chill ambiguity of Patricia Highsmith. But when I discovered that the author of the Maigret series – whom I knew chiefly through the BBC adaptations with Rupert Davies – was also the author of stand-alone novels, my expectations of the genre changed and expanded. These books belonged more alongside Camus and Sartre than Arthur Conan Doyle. The popular joke in *Canard Enchaîné* that 'M. Simenon makes his living by killing someone every month and then discovering the murderer' seemed nothing more than that. A joke.

It's symptomatic of our misunderstanding of the unique Georges Simenon that so many people believe he was French. In fact, he was Belgian, born in Liège in 1903 and brought up in a poorly defined country which had often suffered under occupation. In Belgium, few people fostered illusions about national greatness. 'Under occupation,' he wrote, 'your overwhelming concern is with what you will eat.' Simenon's background, and his lifelong feeling that he was disliked by his mother, left him with the aim of developing, equally as a writer and as a man, a wholly undeluded view of life. As he later observed, 'It must be great to belong to a group, a nation, a class. It would give you a feeling of superiority. If you're alone you're not superior to anyone.' Or, as he put it rather more bitterly: 'During earthquakes and wars and floods and shipwrecks you see a love between men that you don't see at any other time.'

In fact, he could hardly have been less French. What Frenchman or woman would speak of their loathing of gastronomy – 'all that terrible fussing about what you eat'? What French writer or politician would agree that 'Every ideal ends in a fierce struggle against those who do not share it?' Simenon was particularly horrified by Charles de Gaulle's pretence that the French had won the war. The untruth offended him. Simenon believed the events of the 1930s and 1940s had defeated the French as thoroughly as they had the Germans. 'I've ceased to believe in evil, only in illness. Nixon believes he's the champion of the United States, de Gaulle the rebuilder of France. Yet nobody locks them up. Those who invent morals, who define them and impose them, end up believing in them. We're all hopeless prisoners of what we choose to believe.'

Simenon, not prone to grand literary statements, once said that he wanted to write like Sophocles or Euripides.

Over and again, he describes someone quietly living their life, until some random *fait divers* – a road accident, a heart attack, an inheritance – brings out a fatal element in their character which trips them up. Striking out towards freedom, they fall instead into captivity. He had the idea that a book, like a Greek play, should be experienced in a single session. 'You can't see a tragedy in more than one sitting.' Serial killers, soon to become the thundering clichés of modern drama, whether speaking Danish, Swedish or English, would have held no appeal for Simenon precisely because they are, by definition, extraordinary - and considerably less common in life than on television. Typically, in one of Simenon's stories, a single crime is enough to ensure that a hitherto normal life falls apart, with no notice, as though any of us might at any time suddenly encounter a crisis which we will turn out to be powerless to overcome.

The thrill of reading a novel, said Simenon, is to 'look through the keyhole to see if other people have the same feelings and instincts you do'. The man who, when adolescent, says he suffered physical pain at the idea that there could be so many women who would escape him, has the intense focus of a voyeur. An ex-journalist, he often describes towns from their canals or railway lines, because from there you could look into the back of residents' lives and not be deceived by the front. He may have said, 'Other people collect stamps, I collect human beings,' but remarkably he refuses at all times to pass judgement on anyone. 'You will find no priests in my work!' Not only does Simenon take care to exclude politics, religion, history and philosophy from his character's dialogue and thoughts, but the deadpan flatness of his prose style and his bare-bone vocabulary create a disturbing absence of moral control. 'Fifty years ago people had answers, now they don't.'

It was this fallen universe of compromise that I found so convincing as an adolescent. It matched what I had already seen of life. I knew at first hand that Simenon was right when he said that 'the criminal is often less guilty than his victim'. But it was only when I was older that I became addicted to the hard stuff – the unsparing novels which take his fatalistic view to its ultimate. If, as is generally thought, Simenon wrote around four hundred books, then about 117 are serious novels, the *romans durs* which meant most to him. André Gide, one of his many literary admirers, when asked which of Simenon's books a beginner should read first, famously replied 'All of them.' But to my own taste, Simenon's most searching work came out of his queasy, compromised time in occupied France, and in his desperate hunt thereafter for personal happiness in heavy-drinking exile in the United States. If you want to read three of his greatest books, try the deceptively light *Sunday*, written in 1958 about a Riviera hotel-keeper who spends a year preparing to kill his wife; try *The Widow*, published, like *The Outsider*, in 1942, and at least equal to Camus' work in portraying a doomed and alienated life; and above all be sure to read *Dirty Snow*, a story of petty crime and killing at a time of collaboration in a country which remains unnamed, but which is always taken to be France under the Nazis.

Because he was foolish enough in an interview to claim to have slept with ten thousand women – the real figure, said his third wife, rather crisply, was nearer 1,200 – Simenon has sometimes been accused of misogyny, just as by allowing films to be made of his books at the Berlin-supervised Continental Studios in Vichy France during the war, he was also accused of collaboration. The charge of misogyny at least is unfair. A small man's fear of women is often his subject, and he describes that fear with his usual pitiless accuracy. In his books, casual sex is fine, it may or may not be satisfying, but passion is always dangerous because it arouses feelings neither party can control – and loss of control is seen to be a particularly masculine terror. In these circumstances, sex comes closer to despair than to joy. The women he portrays are not usually manipulative or cruel or deceitful. Far from it. They simply possess an inadvertent power to disturb men and to drive them mad. They exercise this power more often in spite of themselves then deliberately. All of his books are, in one way or another, about power of different kinds, and he specialises in depicting the lives of those near the bottom of society – the concierges and the salespeople, the waiters and the clerks – who possess very little. No wonder, when he went to America, that he remarked how everyone was expected to have a hobby, so that in one small field at least they might exercise a measure of domination.

The inspiration for finally deciding to write a play from Simenon came from my friend Bill Nighy who knew that I was a fan. He gave me a present of a rare first edition of a novel which had been almost entirely forgotten. Even now, I have yet to meet anyone in Britain who claims to have read *La Main*. In Moura Budberg's translation, long out of print, the book had been published as *The Man on the Bench in the Barn*. It was written in 1968, but its atmosphere clearly derived from Simenon's own period of residence in Connecticut, where he moved to live with his new wife, Denyse Ouimet, in the late 1940s. In the book, the town he then lived in, Lakeville, is renamed Brentwood. His house, Shadow Rock Farm, becomes fictionally Yellow Rock Farm, but the topography and feel of the place are pretty much identical, with beavers playing in a nearby stream, and the local Connecticut community expecting strong but obsolescent standards of private morality. The only detail omitted was Simenon's own telephone number: Hemlock 5.

We hear a lot about Henry James and the American's traditional fascination with Europe. We hear rather less about its opposite. In my view, there is something rare and interesting artistically when a European sensibility engages with American morals. *La Main* describes America at a point of change, when the suburban world patrolled so brilliantly by writers like Richard Yates, Sloan Wilson and Patricia Highsmith is about to yield to a newer way of life, theoretically freer but equally treacherous. It was characteristic of Simenon to suspect that sexual liberation might not deliver everything it promised. After all, he doubted everything, except his own writing. But it was even more characteristic of him to be in the right place, as he had been in France and Africa before the war, and at the right time, equipped with a reporter's calm genius for putting a moment in a bottle.

David Hare
September 2016

The Red Barn, produced in association with Scott Rudin, was first performed in the Lyttelton auditorium of the National Theatre, London, on 6 October 2016. The cast, in order of appearance, was as follows:

Ingrid Dodd Hope Davis
Dr Warren Stuart Milligan
Mona Sanders Elizabeth Debicki
Ray Sanders Nigel Whitmey
Donald Dodd Mark Strong
Patricia Ashbridge Anna Skellern
Lieutenant Olsen Oliver Alvin-Wilson
Janet Jade Yourell
Mr Dodd Michael Elwyn

Director Robert Icke
Designer Bunny Christie
Lighting Designer Paule Constable
Sound Designer Tom Gibbons

Characters

Ingrid Dodd
Donald Dodd
Mona Sanders

Ray Sanders
Dr Warren
Patricia Ashbridge
Lieutenant Olsen
Janet
Mr Dodd

THE RED BARN

'The puppet still worked, but I had cut the strings
and no one pulled them any longer.'

Georges Simenon, *La Main*

PART ONE: DONALD

PART TWO: MONA

PART THREE: INGRID

Part One: Donald

ONE

Lakeville, Connecticut. Saturday, 25 January 1969. The stage is a dark square. Dim at first, then clear, at the very back, coming out of the darkness like an illusion, the projected image of a retina, huge, the detail of the eye complete. Then near the front, a woman in a padded chair, her eyes hidden by complex optical technology. Ingrid Dodd is forty, tall, fair-haired and calm. Dr Warren, fifty, is looking into them. Then he turns the lights on.

Dr Warren I don't think you've anything to worry about. Your sight's perfect. You see everything.

He removes the machinery. Her eyes are green.

Your eyes are in perfect shape, Mrs Dodd.

Ingrid I was worried.

Dr Warren No need to be.

Ingrid My father suffered from glaucoma.

Dr Warren What did your father do?

Ingrid He was a surgeon.

Dr Warren Tell me your maiden name. Remind me.

Ingrid Whitaker.

Dr Warren Ah yes. Dr Irving Whitaker. What a privilege. To be the daughter of such a great man.

Ingrid gathers up her coat and handbag.

When we look for glaucoma, we expect the retinal ganglion cells to be in a characteristic pattern of loss. We look for ocular hypertension, raised intraocular pressure, increased aqueous humour. There's no sign of any of those.

Ingrid It's called the silent thief of sight, isn't it?

Dr Warren Yes.

Ingrid Because you don't notice it happening.

Dr Warren May I?

He hands her remaining shopping bag.

Ingrid Thank you.

Dr Warren There's no such thing as perfect sight. But for a person of your age, yours is as good as it gets.

He shakes her hand.

You're a very fortunate woman, Mrs Dodd.

TWO

The stage expands and heightens to turn into a massive snowstorm. A driving blizzard and howling winds. The noise is tremendous. Through the snow comes the beam of a flashlight. Three figures are fighting their way through the snow. One of them is Ingrid, who is holding hands with Mona Sanders. She is thirty-eight, very small, dark, sensual, weighs next to nothing. Behind them comes Donald Dodd. He is forty-five. All three are dressed in smart, regular winter coats, which are inadequate for the conditions.

Mona Can anyone see Ray?

Ray Yes, I'm here.

A fourth figure appears. Ray, like Donald, is forty-five, but slightly more imposing, with brown hair.

Donald Ray, keep close! Come on, everyone, stick together, stick together! It isn't far.

Ray I can't see. I can't see anything!

Donald Then take hold of my hand.

The two women are making headway at the front. Ray takes hold of Donald.

Stay close! Stick close! Stick with me.

Ray Donald, you're letting go!

Donald I'm here. I'm right here. I'm right beside you.

Ray Where's your hand?

The flashlight flickers and goes out. Driving snow. The storm becomes deafening.

Ingrid What's happened?

Donald The flashlight's gone. You go ahead, we'll follow you.

Ingrid Mona, are you all right?

Mona I'm fine, I'm making it.

Donald Stay up ahead

Mona Is Ray with Donald?

Ingrid Yes. I think so. I can't see anything.

Mona Where's the house?

Ingrid It must be close.

The two women disappear. Donald has turned round and is looking for Ray.

Donald Ray! Ray! Where are you? I can't see you. Where are you?

The distant sound of Ray's voice: 'I'm here. I'm over here!'

Donald Where? Where? WHERE?

Only Donald is visible now. He is standing stock still in the middle of the storm.

Ray? Where are you? Ray?

The snow thickens. White-out.

THREE

The living room of Yellow Rock Farm. A well-appointed clapboard house. The door opens and in comes Ingrid. She is covered in snow, and barely able to breathe. She goes to turn on the lights. The sound of the switch clicking. She tries several times. Everything's out. The only light is from outside the windows and from the embers of a fire burning in the grate. Just behind Ingrid in comes Mona, also covered in snow, completely exhausted.

There you are.

Mona Thank God.

Ingrid You made it.

Mona I was close. I kept close.

Ingrid I can't breathe. Even now.

Mona I know. It's –

Ingrid Every time I breathe it's like –

Mona Where are the men? Did you see the men?

Ingrid Swallowing a sword. They were just behind.

Mona I haven't heard Ray.

Ingrid Ray was there. Hold on, someone's coming. It looks like Donald.

Donald comes in.

Donald Are you there? Are you safe?

Mona Yes.

Ingrid You're alone.

Donald My God, that's the worst I've ever seen. It's been bad, but never –

Mona Have you seen Ray?

Donald Not in the last –

Ingrid I think we were out there for an hour.

Donald is clicking vainly at the light switch. Ingrid calls through the house.

Ingrid Ray! Ray!

Donald We need a light.

Ingrid The power's out.

Donald We're going to need heat. Whatever happens, we need to stay warm.

Donald goes back to the door.

Mona Donald, we shouldn't close the door.

Donald We have to close the door. We'll freeze to death if it's open.

Ingrid Ray's still out there.

Mona Where is he?

Donald He should be here. I don't know why he isn't. He was beside me.

The women have collapsed on the sofas. Donald goes back to the open door.

Ray! Ray! Where are you? We're here!

At once Ingrid gets up.

Ingrid I'm going to get the candles. I know where they are. They're out the back.

Donald (*at door*) This way!

He turns to explain to Mona.

He was just behind me.

Mona You said beside.

Donald No, behind.

Ingrid has gone out, groping her way to the kitchen.

Ray! Ray! Are you out there? Where are you? Ray!

He turns back to Mona.

Beside to begin with, and then behind. I told him to hold my hand, but he let go.

Mona Yes, but where is he?

Donald Ray! Ray!

He gives up, closing the door. He moves into the room. He kneels down by the grate to re-animate the fire.

He'll be here soon. My God, there was a moment back there when even I –

Mona How far did we come?

Donald Maybe less than a mile. From when the Chrysler got stuck.

Mona It felt like more. I couldn't see anything.

Ingrid returns with candles. One of them is already lit.

8

Ingrid Well?

Donald Well what?

Ingrid Is Ray back?

Donald He isn't back yet.

Ingrid waits.

Ingrid He ought to be.

Donald Yes.

Ingrid By now.

There is a silence, Ingrid not moving.

Ingrid Well? What do you think?

Donald I think I should go and get him.

Ingrid That's what I think.

Donald OK. I need a drink first.

Ingrid You don't think –

Donald What? Say it.

But Ingrid says nothing.

Mona Are you going back out?

Donald I'll have a whisky for the cold. And then I'll head right out.

Relieved, Ingrid now moves round the room placing candles all over and lighting them.

Ingrid I'm sure that's right. That's the right thing to do.

Mona You don't think it's dangerous?

Ingrid I think we have to. We can't leave him. You can't find the house if you don't know where it is.

Donald I'll have a whisky and then I'll go out.

But he doesn't move. Ingrid breaks off from candles and goes to the door.

Ingrid I'll get your things.

Donald There are gloves at the door.

Ingrid I've got them.

Donald The parka.

Ingrid I have it.

Ingrid has returned with an armful of clothes. Donald starts to add layers.

More scarves. Put this on your head.

Donald I'm going to look ridiculous.

Donald pulls on a woollen bonnet, then sits down to pull on boots.

I'm going to work out a system.

Ingrid Good.

Donald Set about it systematically.

Ingrid That sounds good.

Donald Head back the way we came.

Ingrid Find the car?

Donald Then start to circle. That's the plan.

Ingrid You're going to widen out?

Donald nods.

Donald All right, forget the whisky, I'd better get on with it.

Ingrid You'll need batteries for the flashlight. They're in the kitchen.

Donald goes out to get them.

Don't worry, Mona, I'm sure Ray's fine.

She lights more candles. The room is beginning to glow.

Ingrid What you need is a hot bath. You need to get out of your clothes. I'm going to get you a robe.

Mona Thank you. I'm going to put this chair by the fire.

Ingrid Do that. And I'll start the bath.

Ingrid goes. Mona moves a chair, then takes off her coat. Underneath she has a dazzling scarlet dress. She unzips it. She has a slip on. She calls through before Ingrid returns.

Mona I had no idea.

Ingrid (*off*) How could you? You've never been in Lakeville in January.

Mona You said you listened to the forecast.

Ingrid (*off*) I came back from Dr Warren. I listened in the car.

She returns with a thick sweater and a dressing gown.

The storm wasn't expected until tomorrow.

She hands the clothes to Mona.

If you remember, I tried to get Donald to leave.

Mona Everyone was having a good time.

Ingrid That's Harold Ashbridge for you. He gives a good party.

Mona He can afford to.

Ingrid But I looked out at one point. I thought: we ought to leave. I've lived here all my life. I've learned to respect the weather.

Mona rallies a little.

Mona Ray's going to be furious –

Ingrid I'm sure.

Mona When he gets back. Whatever happens, we're snowed in.

Ingrid Probably for days.

Mona He has important meetings back in Manhattan.

Ingrid does not react.

Do you think Donald will be out there for long?

Ingrid If he gets lucky, he'll be back in five minutes. If not, he could be out there for hours.

Mona It's so good of him.

Ingrid Yes. Yes, sometimes you have to push him, but Donald always does the right thing.

Donald returns. He's now dressed from head to toe in thick clothes, his face almost hidden except for his eyes.

Donald So. Here we are.

Mona It's good of you, Donald.

Donald Don't be ridiculous.

Mona Even so. You're a good man.

Donald If only.

There is a moment.

Mona I'm really grateful to you.

Ingrid Good luck, Donald. Good luck out there.

He goes out.

Mona I'll have the bath.

Mona goes out swiftly. Ingrid is left standing.

FOUR

Donald comes out of the front door of the house. The storm is even more powerful than before. He closes the door, and then he takes a few steps and stands listening. He takes a few more steps and then he stops. The sound of a barn door banging insistently. He stands completely still, then reaches in his pocket to take out a cigarette. He lights it. He stands, remembering, and as he does, the noise of the storm dies and is replaced by a woman's voice.

Patricia (*voice*) I was a model. I was a model for a while. I did modelling work. Don't get me wrong, not on the catwalk or anything like that. I was in the catalogues. Those big books that come through the door and land with a thump.

FIVE

Patricia Ashbridge is at the party. She's thirty, playful, overt, with plunging neckline. She has a drink in her hand, and seems quite far gone. She's talking to Ingrid, who is in her evening dress, formal, statuesque. There is the sound of a lively, heavy-drinking crowd.

Patricia There was I. Playing with a beach ball. And smiling. My teeth were dazzling.

Ingrid Do they do those things in the studio? Or do they shoot them on location? I've always wondered. The sand, is that for real? Or are you in some sort of – I don't know – sandbox?

Patricia Oh both. We did both. Sometimes Coney Island standing in for the Caribbean.

Ray approaches, drink in hand. He's in a smart suit.

Ingrid Ray, have you met Harold's new wife? Patricia Ashbridge, Ray Sanders. Ray Sanders, Patricia Ashbridge.

Ray Actually we met.

Patricia We met a few drinks ago.

Ray Back in the early martinis.

They laugh.

Patricia No, we're joking –

Ray We were already acquainted.

Ray Patricia and I met a few years back.

Patricia Just briefly. We knew each other.

Ray True!

Patricia We first met at Los Angeles airport.

Ray We took the red-eye together. That's how we first met.

Patricia 'Fly me to the moon and let me play among the stars . . .'

Ray We shared a scotch for every state we passed over.

Patricia Quickest flight I ever took.

Ingrid is looking, puzzled by their behaviour.

Patricia In fact, I promised Ray I'd show him the house.

14

Ray I'd love that. Have you redecorated?

Patricia Me? Redecorate?

Ray Since you married Harold?

Patricia Do you know, I haven't? Believe it or not.

Ray I'd have thought that's the first thing you'd do.

Patricia I take things as they come.

Ray You're not threatened?

Patricia Not in the slightest. I'm Wife Number Three. I'm living in another woman's taste and it's making me very happy.

They're looking deeply at each other. Ingrid can't think of anything to say. Patricia turns back to Ingrid.

I couldn't believe it was Ray. Of all places. In Lakeville. I never thought I'd see him again.

Ray It's me.

Patricia And it's pure chance.

Ray I was telling Patricia how we'd been on a road trip in Canada. And so it just seemed a wonderful idea. I called. When was it?

Ingrid Wednesday.

Ray That's right. Wednesday. I just thought, go see my old friend Donald. Spur of the moment.

Patricia I'm glad you did.

Ray And see Ingrid of course. We were in Quebec City. Have you been there?

Patricia Never.

Ray It's worth it. It really is.

Ingrid is watching now, trying to de-code.

Patricia Do you still fly to LA?

Ray Oh sure. You?

Patricia You're going to hate me. We only fly out of Teterboro.

Ray Ah. You're strictly private nowadays?

Patricia I'm always in Harold's personal crate.

Ray Don't you miss the rough and tumble of public transport?

Patricia I miss the rough and the tumble. In that order.

Ray You should try it again.

Patricia Do you know, I think I might?

She sets off, putting her hand on Ray's back.

Skip this way, Ray, and I'll take you on the tour. Do you want to come?

Ingrid I've seen it.

She does a little hand-wave at Ingrid as they leave.

Patricia See you later.

They go. Ingrid stares straight ahead, taking in what she has seen, then walks suddenly away. The music is louder.

SIX

The Yellow Rock living room. Mona is staring into the fire, which is now blazing. Donald comes back through the front door and sees her on the sofa.

Donald Ingrid?

Mona No, it's not Ingrid. It's Mona. I'm wearing her robe. She lent me her robe.

There is a silence.

He isn't with you? You didn't find him?

Donald No.

Mona You were away so long.

Donald I know.

Mona Over two hours. I began to realise – the longer you were gone –

Donald Not necessarily –

Mona It's not good though, is it?

Donald It's neither good nor bad.

Mona It's bad.

Donald Where's Ingrid?

Mona She's making something to eat.

Donald OK.

Mona Did she say sandwiches?

Donald If I were you, I wouldn't – I'm saying – Ray is strong. He's much stronger than me. Fitter. He'll have found a place to shelter.

Mona But you didn't find it.

Mona looks away.

Donald I shouldn't worry. Ray has an instinct for survival. At Yale – from day one – I saw him across the square. I thought, 'This is a guy who can look after himself.' He had an air.

Mona Did he?

Donald He'll hunker down somewhere safe till the storm passes.

Mona just looks at him.

Mona You should take off those clothes.

Ingrid comes in with a plate of thick sandwiches.

Ingrid It's important Mona eats.

Donald Essential.

Ingrid She had a bath while the water was still hot.

She puts her hand on the radiator.

They're cooling already. Feel.

Donald nods in acknowledgement.

I guess you haven't had any luck. Did you see anything at all –

Donald Nothing –

Ingrid That might – anything that would suggest –

Donald No. I didn't see anything.

Ingrid You went back to the car?

Donald I reckon it's a mile. Started over from there.

Ingrid No sign?

Donald You have to remember: our footsteps were covered behind us as soon as we walked. If he tripped for instance – if he tripped on a rock – that's always a danger here –

Ingrid puts down the sandwiches.

Ingrid We're going to need more wood.

Donald You tried the phone?

Ingrid Of course. The lines are down.

Donald That's good.

Ingrid Good? Why is it good?

Donald Because if he's at a neighbour's, he can't call. Ray can't call us even if he wants to.

Mona I see what you're saying.

Donald (*to Ingrid*) No, thank you.

He starts to take off his outer clothes.

Ingrid So strange. Why did he let go?

Donald Let go?

Ingrid Of your hand?

Donald Oh . . .

Ingrid We kept saying, it's essential we hold on. It's the only way to survive.

Mona I was hanging on to Ingrid for dear life.

Donald I don't know why he let go. Both of us have the leader's instinct. The boy scout thing. Ray and me. Both of us think we know best perhaps. We like to lead.

There's a short silence.

Ingrid He was enjoying the party, wasn't he?

Mona The party?

Ingrid Before.

Mona At the Ashbridges'? I think he enjoyed it. Why do you ask that?

Ingrid No. If he was – if he –

Mona What?

Ingrid No, what I'm saying, I didn't see much of him.

Donald It's a big house.

Ingrid He had a good time?

Donald Seemed to. Yes. From what I saw.

He shifts, uneasy. Ingrid is watching him.

I could manage a drink.

Ingrid Now you can have one.

Donald goes over and pours himself a whisky. He lifts his glass in an odd toast.

Donald Mona, here's to your good health.

Donald drinks, then makes a formal statement.

I want to say, in the circumstances: if you feel we should have left the party earlier –

Mona No one feels that.

Donald I don't want you to feel –

Mona No one does.

Donald You'd say if –

Mona Honestly.

Donald We did discuss it, if you remember.

Mona No one blames you, Donald.

Donald Thank you.

Ingrid waits, but Donald doesn't move.

Ingrid Look to the fire, Donald.

Donald I'm on it.

Ingrid So can you get the wood?

Donald puts down his glass. Then he rolls back a corner of the carpet. He pulls up a trapdoor which leads down the cellar. He takes the flashlight, and walks down the steps. He disappears down beneath the floor.

We won't get the power back for a while.

Mona It's happened before?

Ingrid Oh yes.

Mona I don't think we should go to bed.

Ingrid We can't.

Mona It seems wrong to go to bed. In the circumstances.

Ingrid We should wait here. Till Ray gets back.

Mona It's hard. It all seems so unreal.

Ingrid We have to keep warm and we have to eat. I'm going to get a coffee pot and heat it on the fire.

Donald is returning from below, his arms full of logs. Ingrid goes out. Mona has sprawled in a chair. She's unkempt, her hair wild. She seems muzzy, abandoned.

Mona She's wonderful, isn't she?

Donald Yes.

Mona That calm she has.

Donald It's a sort of serenity.

Mona Yes.

Donald She's always had it.

Mona Her father was a surgeon?

Donald And her mother was a Clayburn. Old American stock.

Mona You're lucky.

Donald Oh, I know I'm lucky.

Mona I'd have called myself lucky until just now.

Donald is kneeling by the fire, adding to it.

Donald Ray said you'd had an unsettled childhood.

Mona I was brought up in the theatre.

Donald Ray mentioned that.

Mona Dad wrote musicals.

Donald He said you lived on the road.

Mona We lived in hotels. Out of town.

Donald With your mother?

Mona No. She wasn't around. When I grew up, I was an actress for a while. Then I met Ray.

Donald What kind of actress?

Mona Oh, comedy. Sexy comedy, really.

They smile.

Donald Is that how you met Ray?

Mona No. Ray was at all those parties. There were a lot of parties in those days. Business parties.

Donald In Manhattan?

Mona Businessmen liked to have actresses on their arm. You know how it is. Show them off.

Donald Did you mind that?

Mona Never. Why should I?

Donald Oh, I don't know.

Mona I saw Ray several times. It was months before he spoke to me.

Donald He was biding his time.

Mona Maybe.

Donald Planning.

Mona looks thoughtful a moment.

Mona I'd come out of an affair which had hurt me badly. Ray nursed me out of it. You don't forget kindness like that.

Donald is still kneeling by the fire.

I know what you've done.

Donald What I've done?

Mona Tonight.

Donald What have I done?

Mona I don't underestimate it. You risked your life for him. In that weather.

Donald Oh.

Mona Well, you did.

Donald That isn't quite true.

Mona Going out again when you didn't need to. To go again.

Donald We're best friends since college. Anyone would have done the same.

He looks at her, not knowing what to say.

Mona Be careful. Your sleeve's falling in the fire.

Donald looks down. He has rested his hand too close. He takes it away.

Donald Listen.

Mona What am I listening to?

Donald The wind's dying. It's a good sign. We're on the way back.

Ingrid comes in with a coffee pot.

Ingrid It may be days till we're out of here, but that's still a good sign, did you hear it?

Mona Yes.

Ingrid The wind dropping. The worst may be over. As soon as the phones are back, we call the neighbours.

She sets the pot down. Mona is looking all the time at Donald.

Have something to eat. Ham. Ham and cheese –

Mona I don't know how to tell you. I don't know how to convince you. I don't want to eat.

Ingrid Mona –

Mona I really don't. I want to wait until Ray is safe. Why don't we at least try and sleep?

Ingrid The bedrooms are freezing cold.

Donald Mona's right. We're all exhausted. I agree.

Ingrid turns to Donald, not put off her stride by Mona's outburst.

Ingrid Donald, there are mattresses in the girls' rooms. If we lay them out.

Donald goes out silently.

Mona The girls are at school?

Ingrid That's right. They're at Adams. In Litchfield.

Mona Is that far?

Ingrid It's one of the better schools in Connecticut.

Mona Is that your old school?

Ingrid Yes. That's why we chose it.

Mona How long have they been gone?

Ingrid Mildred's fifteen. Cecilia's twelve.

Mona You must miss them.

Ingrid It's different. It's different now we're alone. That was one phase, this is another.

Donald comes back with two light, narrow mattresses and sets them out, side by side, feet to the fire.

I suggest you put them by the fire.

Donald OK.

Ingrid That's the best idea.

Donald I'll get another from the guest room.

He goes out at once. Ingrid arranges them with very slight gaps between them.

Ingrid Side by side, I think, don't you?

Mona Perfect.

Ingrid Like sardines. We'll sleep in a row.

Donald is back with a third mattress.

Donald Here we are.

Ingrid I'll get blankets.

Donald Thanks.

She goes out. Mona has not moved. She is sitting completely still, watching as Donald lays out the third mattress, equidistant, the smallest of gaps between. Then:

Mona I hope you'll come by when this is all over.

Donald I'd like that.

Mona Both of us would love to see you. You're always welcome. Ray's fond of you, you know.

Donald It's true. I don't get to Manhattan enough. Ingrid never. She has a lot to do. Clubs. Charities. She's out doing good work.

He fusses over the mattresses. Mona is still watching, silent.

You won't get her to New York. She's happier here.

They look at each other. Then Ingrid comes back in with blankets. She smiles at them, calm, and then goes and puts blankets down on each mattress. Mona gets up and walks across to the mattress on the right and lies down.

Mona Thank you, Ingrid.

She takes a blanket and covers herself. Donald has taken off his shoes.

Ingrid You go in the middle, Donald.

Donald takes the middle mattress and lies down, and Ingrid goes on the left. After a few moments, Mona

turns on her side, facing in. And a few moments later,
Donald turns on his side, facing Mona. Mona's hand is
outside the blanket, by her side. Donald stares at it.
Mona has fallen asleep. Donald closes his eyes. Ingrid
is still.

Part Two: Mona

SEVEN

Darkness. The sound of a phone conversation.

Donald (*voice*) This is Donald Dodd of Lakeville.

Olsen (*voice*) The lawyer?

Donald (*voice*) Yes.

Olsen (*voice*) I know you, Mr Dodd. This is Lieutenant Olsen.

Donald (*voice*) I have to report a disappearance. Last night – no, it was the night before, we went to a party at the Ashbridges'.

Olsen (*voice*) Yes, I know.

Donald (*voice*) You know?

Olsen (*voice*) Yes.

Donald (*voice*) On the way back we got stuck in the snow. It was only when we got to the house, I noticed my friend was gone.

A silence.

Are you there?

Olsen (*voice*) I'm listening, Mr Dodd.

Donald (*voice*) His name is Ray Sanders of Miller and Sanders, the public relations firm.

Olsen (*voice*) I'm going to come out when I can. It isn't snowploughs we need, it's bulldozers. Call me up if you have any news.

EIGHT

Day. The living room of Yellow Rock Farm, restored to order. It's Monday and it looks as if nothing has happened. The snow is dazzlingly white outside the windows. Donald is at the door, letting in Lieutenant Olsen, tall, impassive, with a crew-cut. Ingrid has laid out coffee and cake and is sitting, immaculate, waiting.

Donald Lieutenant, well done, you made it.

Olsen Mr Dodd.

Donald At last. I'm sorry to get you out. You must be very busy.

Donald shakes his head. Ingrid gets up to shake Olsen's hand.

Ingrid Lieutenant . . .

Olsen Mrs Dodd . . .

Ingrid I called Mona down. I'm afraid she was asleep.

Olsen Really? Has she been sleeping a lot?

Mona comes in, fresh from bed. She has pulled on slacks and a blouse and has bare feet.

Ah Mrs Sanders, I'm Lieutenant Olsen. Why don't you sit down over there?

Ingrid I can find you some slippers.

Mona I'm fine. Really.

She sits and tucks her legs up again under her. Olsen gets out a police notebook.

Olsen As I understand it, you're married to Ray Sanders, you live on Sutton Place in New York, and he's a partner in a public relations firm.

Mona He's a lawyer, he was their legal adviser originally.

Olsen So you were on your way through Lakeville, going somewhere else?

Donald They were going home. They'd been vacationing in Canada.

Olsen You told me, Mr Dodd, that you took your friends to the Ashbridges'?

Donald You know how it is, every year old Ashbridge gives a party before he goes to Florida, he doesn't mind who comes along . . .

Olsen smiles, familiar with Ashbridge.

Olsen Did your husband have a lot to drink?

Mona I wasn't with him for most of the time.

Olsen He was talking to other people?

Mona It was that kind of occasion. He probably drank quite a bit.

Olsen And you, Mr Dodd?

Donald Me?

Ingrid is looking closely at Donald.

Not to begin with, but maybe later in the evening.

Olsen Something happened?

Donald Sorry?

Olsen To make you change your behaviour?

Donald Oh. No, nothing. Really.

Olsen Nothing? Or nothing really?

Donald Nothing.

Donald throws a look to Ingrid.

Mona Ray and Harold got into a conversation in the corner. They were discussing business.

Olsen What sort of business?

Mona Well –

She looks slightly desperately to Donald.

Donald I don't need to tell you Ashbridge is one of the richest men in America. He owns stores. Television stations. Even mines, I think.

Olsen OK.

Donald And Ray's in public relations.

Olsen So?

Donald They'd never met. Wham! It was like that. Two businessmen who'd always wanted to meet. They took each other's numbers. I'd say Harold was on the point of offering him work.

Olsen I see. And after that –

Mona Yes?

Olsen You'd say your husband was behaving normally?

Mona looks to Donald, nervous.

Mona I'm wondering why you're asking this question.

Olsen When there's a disappearance –

Mona But this is an accident –

Olsen I don't doubt it.

Mona Surely?

Olsen Or in cases of suicide –

Mona Is that what you're thinking?

Olsen There are routine questions. Did your husband have any reason to kill himself?

Mona No.

Olsen Do you have children?

Mona No.

Olsen How long have you been married?

Mona Six years.

Olsen Did your husband meet anyone he had known before at the Ashbridges'?

Donald shifts slightly, uneasy.

Mona Not that I know of.

Olsen A woman?

Mona I saw him talking to many women. He's always very popular.

Olsen Was there a particular incident that comes to your mind? A quarrel?

Mona blushes. Donald is alert. She's thrown.

Mona Ingrid, I wonder if I could have a glass of water.

Ingrid Of course.

Olsen Anything out of the ordinary? Anything unusual?

Ingrid goes to get water.

Think.

Mona I'm thinking.

Mona shakes her head.

Olsen And you were among the last to leave?

Donald I guess we stayed on longer than most.

Olsen And after you'd abandoned the car, you walked on in the dark?

Donald Tried to. I wouldn't say 'walked'. Our legs went deep into the snow.

Ingrid returns with a glass of water. Olsen is writing in his book.

Mona Thank you.

Olsen Was it difficult to find the house?

Donald I literally bumped into it.

Olsen And where was Mr Sanders at that point?

Donald Well that's it. I'd been calling out to him.

Olsen And then?

Donald Then when he didn't make it, I went out to look for him.

He looks to the women for confirmation, but they show no reaction.

Olsen You went off alone?

Donald Yes.

Olsen Did you go back to the car?

Donald Yes.

Olsen It was empty of course? And the barn?

Donald stares at him.

Donald Sorry?

Olsen The barn? Did you go the barn? I saw a red barn. It's yours, isn't it? It's your barn?

Donald Yes.

Olsen Did you check he wasn't there?

Donald Yes. I checked in the barn.

Olsen makes a note. Ingrid shifts, staring at him.

Olsen So you went in?

Donald I think I did.

Olsen Did you or didn't you?

Donald I think I did. I called inside, but there was no reply.

Olsen gets up and gestures towards the window.

Olsen I've got a steam shovel working out there. If you look out the window, we're putting up an arc light. Means we can carry on for a while.

Donald In the dark?

Olsen You never know. We're a long way from knowing what happened.

Donald follows him to the door.

Donald Thank you, Lieutenant. Everyone here really appreciates what you're doing.

Olsen I'll be in touch.

They shake hands, and Donald closes the door. Silently, with no explanation, Mona gets up and walks out of the room.

Ingrid We never had coffee.

She reaches out and pours herself a cup of coffee.

What did you make of him?

Donald Who?

Ingrid The lieutenant.

Donald He has the reputation of being good at his job.

Ingrid He knew a lot, didn't he? Before he came?

Donald It was like he'd already talked to the people at the party. Before he talked to us.

Ingrid But why?

Ingrid throws a glance towards the bedrooms.

I don't know what's going on. I don't believe Mona is suffering –

Donald You mean –

Ingrid Just from observation. The way she behaves.

Donald Isn't it that different people –

Ingrid Oh sure –

Donald Anxiety takes people in different ways, according –

Ingrid Sure.

Donald Grief.

Ingrid Sure.

Donald I've seen it at work. When people are under pressure – some fall apart, others go quiet. She goes to sleep.

Ingrid You think she's really suffering?

Donald What are you asking? I don't understand.

Ingrid I'm surprised, that's all.

Donald Why? Why are you surprised?

Ingrid I don't think she's missing him.

Donald And that surprises you?

Ingrid They always seemed so attached to one another.

35

Donald Attached?

Ingrid Yes.

Donald I think they were attached, yes. Weren't they?
They lived their lives together.

Ingrid More than that. It seemed like love.

Donald It was love. They didn't say it wasn't.

*He gets up to take his coffee cup out to the kitchen.
But he stops, frowning at a small plastic bag which is
on a table by the door. He hesitates, then picks it up.*

What are these?

Ingrid Oh I found them.

Donald Clearly.

Ingrid I meant to put them in the garbage, but then the
lieutenant arrived.

Donald Cigarette butts?

Ingrid Yes.

Donald You picked them up?

Ingrid Yes.

Donald Where did you find them?

Ingrid On the floor. In the barn.

Donald You found them in the barn?

Ingrid Yes. I found ten or twelve. Someone had done a
lot of smoking.

Donald stands a moment, not moving.

Donald That's strange.

Ingrid Isn't it? I'll throw them out.

Donald No. Let me.

Ingrid If that's what you'd prefer.

Ingrid goes out. Donald stands a moment staring, and it's the voice of Dr Warren from the party which overlaps.

Dr Warren 'The greatest honour history can bestow is the title of peacemaker.' You know who said that? Richard Nixon. The thirty-seventh President. And going to be one of the best.

NINE

The party again. The sound of people talking wildly, Sinatra playing. Dr Warren is standing with a whisky, Ingrid a martini.

Dr Warren You know what I say about Nixon?

Ingrid No. Tell me.

Dr Warren Anybody who wants the presidency that badly probably deserves it.

Dr Warren laughs. Donald appears, carrying a Coca-Cola.

Ingrid Donald, you haven't seen Ray by any chance?

Donald Ray? No. He's around.

Ingrid Just Harold's looking for him, and you know how impatient Ashbridge is when he doesn't get what he wants when he wants it.

Dr Warren and Donald smile.

Donald I'll warn Ray when I see him.

Ingrid goes.

Dr Warren I think Nixon can sort the country out.

Donald You think it needs sorting out?

Dr Warren You think America has a future if it goes hippie, or yippie, or dippy, or whatever?

Donald It's just a rash.

Dr Warren That's what you think, is it?

Donald It's a fashion. It's the young. They've always done it.

Dr Warren Have they? Did you do it?

Donald It'll pass.

Dr Warren I don't know what the word is for you, Donald. 'Sanguine', is it? 'Resigned'? Or just plain submissive? You want to let kids take America down the drain?

Donald I want to let kids do what they want.

Dr Warren And us? Are we now allowed to do anything too?

He looks at Donald contemptuously.

I'm getting another drink. Do you want one?

Donald I'm the driver.

Dr Warren goes. Donald is alone. He lights a cigarette. Then he moves across to a door. He opens it. Inside there is a bathroom. Patricia, dressed, is up on the sink, her legs wrapped round Ray. They are making love. Donald stands a moment with the door open. Patricia can see he is there, and she smiles at him. But Ray's back is turned. Donald closes the door. He goes straight to a table with a bottle of whisky and pours a huge drink. Swallows it. Then Mona comes by.

Mona Donald . . .

Donald Hi, Mona.

Mona You OK?

Donald Yes, fine. I'm enjoying myself. You?

Mona Very much so. Nice party.

> *Mona hovers a moment, but then leaves. Donald looks a moment at her retreating figure. Then he reaches for a bottle, and knocks down another double. Ingrid reappears.*

Ingrid The weather's worse. Much worse. As bad as I've ever seen it. We should have gone home.

TEN

The sound of a radio broadcast: the newscaster reports that the whole of the Northern Seaboard has endured the worst snowstorm of the century. Parts of the country have been isolated, fifteen million people without power. Ten people are known to have died and many more are missing. Now the clear-up has begun.

The living room, again. Mona is sitting on one of the sofas. There is the sound of car drawing up and Donald is at the door, letting Olsen in. He takes off his hat respectfully. Mona gets up.

Olsen My condolences, Mrs Sanders.

Mona Thank you.

Olsen It was exactly as you imagined, Mr Dodd.

Donald What I imagined?

Olsen Yes.

Donald Remind me.

Olsen He lost his way near the rock and slipped. He broke his leg in the fall.

Donald The body's still there?

Olsen Oh yes. We're leaving it till you've paid your respects.

Donald nods slightly, as if he had thought of this.

Donald A drink would do you good, Mona. What about you, Lieutenant?

Olsen shakes his head. Donald goes to pour two scotches.

Olsen Later I'll have the body taken to the mortuary. All you'll have to do then is give the necessary instructions.

Donald gives her the scotch. He puts his arm round her.

Donald Courage, Mona, darling.

Mona is a little taken aback. Then:

Donald You are sweet, Donald. Thank you.

He takes his arm away and raises his glass. Olsen shifts.

Olsen I'm wondering where Mrs Dodd is.

Donald She went shopping. In town. We're out of fresh produce. So she went to get some.

He smiles at Olsen, a little defiant.

Olsen I have to warn you, the press is taking an interest.

Donald The press?

Olsen Yes. The storm is big news. Any fatality, I'm afraid, is going to be in the headlines.

Donald It's not going to be a problem. My father edits

the local paper. He's the proprietor too. He owns it. Has done for years.

Olsen I know your father.

Donald Then you know Dad's not a sensationalist. Rather the opposite.

Olsen Even so.

Donald We can trust him to –

Olsen To what, Mr Dodd?

Donald Trust him to handle things.

Olsen It's not the locals you need to worry about. The nationals'll be on your doorstep. This storm's a big story, and anyone caught up in it. You should prepare yourself.

He nods in deference to Mona.

I'm going to leave. As soon as you've visited the body will be moved. Our job is finished. We withdraw. Mr Dodd.

Donald Lieutenant.

Olsen I'm sorry, Mrs Sanders, that this tragedy had to happen here.

Donald leads Olsen to the door. Mona lights a cigarette. Donald closes the door and comes back.

Mona I can say this to you now we're alone. I keep wondering if Ray didn't do it on purpose.

Donald Deliberately?

Mona Yes.

Donald He committed suicide?

Mona That's not a word I like. He may have given fate a little push.

Donald I'm astonished.

Mona Are you? Why?

Donald You knew him better but I knew him longer.

Mona And?

Donald Never once, in all those years – I never saw anything in Ray which – not for a moment.

Mona just looks at him.

Was he in trouble?

Mona Not in business trouble, no.

Donald He said things were going well.

Mona Beyond his wildest dreams.

Donald Well then. And in his intimate life?

He waits a moment.

Mona?

Mona It's not simple. I don't know how to put it. He and I – well, we were wonderful friends. We hid nothing from each other. It was that kind of – that's how our marriage was.

Donald So?

Mona I'll tell you the truth. What it came down to.

Donald Tell me.

Mona I think he was discontented.

Donald How can Ray have been discontented?

Mona In fact, I know he was.

Donald He had everything.

Mona It may have looked like that. From the outside.

Donald It's how it looked to me.

Mona He felt the opposite. He felt he should have been a proper lawyer, like you. In his eyes, you did everything right.

Donald He was a great success.

Mona Yes. Financially. We live in one of the most beautiful apartments on Sutton Place. Every night we entertain. Why do you think Ray drinks so much? *Drank* so much?

Donald I don't know.

Mona He was sick of it.

Donald Ray?

Mona He was sick of the life. We both drank. One night – you want to know this? He told me how disgusted he was.

Donald Disgusted why?

Mona He said, disgusted with playing the fool.

Mona nods.

Donald Playing the fool?

Mona Yes. He was thinking about his father.

Donald Herbert Sanders. I met him several times at Yale. Palaeontology, wasn't it? Archaeology. He was a book dealer.

Mona That's right.

Donald He had a fantastic collection.

Mona He did indeed. And not just of books. He was terribly attractive.

Donald Yes.

Mona He had a string of women. You could even call them a collection.

Donald Yes, but surely he remarried?

Mona Yes. Eventually. His second wife was a much younger woman. She went out one night. He shot himself. Remember?

Donald Yes.

Mona No letter, no explanation.

She looks at Donald.

She came home. There he was.

Donald I didn't know that.

Mona Slumped down among his books. You see what I'm saying? The most charming man you ever met. On the surface. Girlfriends galore –

Donald Are you saying –

Mona His father shot himself in the head.

Donald It's different. It's completely different.

He is shaking his head, but Mona is becoming more emphatic.

Mona That's why he envied you.

Donald Me? Why would anyone envy me?

Mona You're a good father. You love your children. You weren't going to spend your life –

Donald What? I wasn't going to what?

Mona Do I need to spell it out? Obviously, you know, not to chase women –

Donald Oh –

Mona You chose to settle down. Chose to live out here. He said you chose to live decently.

Donald frowns, bewildered.

Donald Was he making fun of me?

Mona No, of course not. Ray said, let's face it, anyone who chose Ingrid, who could marry her, who could live with her, year in, year out – it was a choice, he said –

Donald Meaning? Meaning what? You've started now, you can't leave it there.

He has raised his voice, insistent. Mona smiles slightly at his concern.

Mona Donald, look, Ingrid's an extraordinary woman. We both know that –

Donald She is.

Mona One look at her – she has high standards. She's incapable of doing anything cheap or low. But that's not all. She expects those standards of others. Well?

Donald nods, assenting.

Mona I've watched you together so often.

Donald And?

Mona Why would anyone choose to live with her if –

Donald If what?

Mona That's what Ray admired. That's why he envied you. You wouldn't have chosen Ingrid if you didn't want to follow those high standards yourself.

Donald moves away, a little lost, trying to make sense of what he's hearing.

A lot of people are frightened of her.

Donald Of Ingrid?

Mona Yes.

Donald 'Frightened''s too strong.

Mona They're intimidated. By her scrutiny. When she looks at you. Sometimes – you must have noticed –

Donald What?

Mona Someone so – with such a clear view –

Donald She's not cold.

Mona I didn't say she was cold. She detects weakness, that's all. When you look in her eyes –

Donald Yes.

Mona Her clear green eyes – Ingrid misses nothing. You see too, but you pretend not to.

Donald Like when?

Mona Like that night when you'd been looking for Ray. What was going on then?

Donald Going on?

Donald is panicking, trying not to show it.

And the girls, too. I've met your girls –

Donald Oh, the girls –

Mona Mildred, is it?

Donald Yes. And Cecilia.

Mona They're fine girls. I can tell you, in New York, girls are worldly by the age of ten. Little minxes. Everything for effect. Whereas, with your girls – it's not just Ingrid's genes, it's yours too.

Donald shrugs, as if it's nothing to do with him.

Ray felt worthless. A life of – I don't know –

Donald Say.

Mona Pills. Alcohol. Instability.

Donald looks down ironically at his own whisky glass.

Donald I don't believe it.

Mona I'm not making it up.

Donald We all have moods.

Mona I lived with him, remember?

They are suddenly intimate. Donald speaks quietly.

Donald I wish I could comfort you. I wish I could comfort you better.

Ingrid has entered silently, carrying shopping bags. She comes into the room.

Ingrid You're still here.

Donald Yes.

Ingrid I thought you'd have gone down to see the body.

Mona We're going. We were waiting for you.

Ingrid I'm sorry, Mona. Let me give you a hug.

She has put down her shopping and crosses the room to embrace Mona.

Mona I wanted us all to go together.

Ingrid Of course. Have you called the undertakers?

Mona Actually, we haven't, no.

She looks a little desperately to Donald for support.

Ingrid Don't worry if it's all too much, we can help.

Mona That's kind.

Ingrid Do you know if there's a will?

Mona Again, I just haven't –

Ingrid Quite. I understand.

Mona I'm not worried for myself.

Ingrid I didn't mean that. Just – these things can be complicated.

Mona I'm sure Ray will have taken care of me. He'll have made provision. I know that. And I know Ray always wanted Donald to be his lawyer.

Ingrid So whatever happens, you're in good hands.

They both smile.

Donald In a private capacity. Please. There's no question of a fee.

Mona I'm going to view the body and then go back to New York.

Ingrid That seems like a good plan.

She throws a glance towards Donald.

Would you like Donald to go with you?

Mona I'm sorry?

Ingrid No, I was thinking – you're going to be alone. You're going to be lonely. That enormous apartment –

Mona The maid'll be there.

Ingrid Even so. If Donald went with you to the city –

Mona Really, I'll be fine.

Ingrid Are you sure?

There's a slight impasse. Donald shifts.

Donald I can do whatever anyone thinks best.

Neither of the women respond. They look at each other.

Ingrid Donald, I wonder can you give Mona your card?

Donald Yes, of course.

Ingrid So that if anything urgent –

Donald I have one here.

He has reached into his wallet and got out a white card.

Higgins and Dodd. Higgins, my partner. We have an answering service. Night and day.

They stand a moment.

Ingrid Everything'll get sorted. Everything'll be fine.

Mona We'll see.

Ingrid Shall we see him now?

Mona nods and goes out.

Mona I'll get my coat.

Ingrid thinks a moment, then moves away.

Ingrid She's going to need looking after.

She goes to the kitchen. Donald stands alone a moment, thinking.

ELEVEN

Darkness. The sound of a phone conversation.

Donald (*voice*) Mona?

Mona (*voice*) Yes?

Donald (*voice*) It's Donald.

Mona (*voice*) Donald?

There's a slight pause.

I took some sleeping pills. I just pace the rooms. I don't know what to do with myself.

Donald (*voice*) I'm here with Ingrid.

Mona (*voice*) OK.

Donald (*voice*) It's Ingrid who suggested I call.

Mona (*voice*) Ingrid?

Donald (*voice*) Yes.

Mona (*voice*) Do say thank you for the thought.

Mona's voice has a touch of irony. She slurs as well.

Donald (*voice*) We hated leaving you at the funeral. We wondered how you were getting on.

Mona (*voice*) I saw you with the Millers. Did you have a word?

Donald (*voice*) Mona, I don't want to impose myself.

Mona (*voice*) Are you free on Monday?

Donald (*voice*) At what time?

Mona (*voice*) Would eleven o'clock suit you?

Donald (*voice*) I'll be there.

TWELVE

Sutton Place. The Sanders apartment. A vast room, looking out on the East River. There is a feeling of space and corridors disappearing into silence. The maid Janet, in a neat black uniform, is answering the door. Donald has a briefcase.

Donald I'm sorry, I'm a little early. Janet, isn't it?

Janet Yes, that's right.

Donald I got an earlier train.

Janet Mrs Sanders is changing, sir.

Donald Then I'll wait.

Donald smiles and comes into the room.

Janet Is there anything I can get you sir?

Donald Nothing.

Janet She knows you're here. I'm sure she won't be long.

Janet disappears down a long corridor. A door at the back is slightly open. Donald sets down his briefcase.

Mona (*off*) Donald, is that you?

Donald Yes.

Mona (*off*) Would you prefer to talk in here?

Donald is thrown, picking up his briefcase to take it into the other room. Then putting it down again. As he moves across to the door, Mona appears, wearing a dark blue house-dress. She holds out her hand, and he takes it. Then he pulls her towards him and they kiss. The kiss deepens and becomes more passionate. They look into each other's eyes.

Mona Let's go in.

Donald Mona –

Mona Come.

She goes into the room. He follows. He closes the door.

THIRTEEN

Sutton Place. The bell rings. Janet walks through quickly and opens the front door. Not much is audible or visible in the darkened corridor, but she soon passes back with a large bunch of flowers. She goes out again down the corridor. Nothing. Then Donald comes out of the bedroom. He's in shirtsleeves and trousers, carrying his shoes. He looks tousled. He goes across to the sofa to put them on. His tie is round his neck. After a while, Mona comes in, also unkempt, in her blue house-dress. She goes to get a cigarette from a silver box.

Donald Forgive me, Mona.

Mona What am I forgiving you for?

Donald I was desperate.

Mona I could see.

Donald Too much?

Mona Of course not. Far from it.

Donald Good.

Mona What's your drink?

Donald The same as yours.

Mona Then scotch.

She goes to a small bar.

I'm sorry if I startled you.

Mona I admit I was surprised.

Donald I thought, if I don't do it now, the whole day will be ridiculous, because I'll spend all our time together thinking of nothing else. That's why –

Mona You mean, get it over?

Donald Not quite. More: it was going to happen, so.

She gives him a scotch and they lift their glasses.

Mona To us, Donald.

Donald To us.

They drink. Mona is apparently casual.

Mona Did Ingrid say anything?

Donald What about?

Mona About your coming to see me.

Donald On the contrary. It was her idea.

Mona What a strange woman she is. I told you I was scared of her. But then for a long time I was a little scared of you.

Donald looks down, smiling.

Donald It was your hand.

Mona My hand?

Donald Yes. That's how it started. That night, when we put the mattresses out . . .

Mona Oh, then.

Donald On the floor. Side by side.

Mona By the fire?

Donald Yes. To sleep. Your hand was lying on the floor. I had this insane desire to touch it. To reach out and touch your hand.

Mona But you do actually like me, Donald, don't you?

Donald Oh yes.

Mona Are you sure?

Donald I like you very much.

Mona is serene, confident. Janet comes in with the flowers, now in a vase.

Mona Who are they from?

Janet A family friend. Wanting to comfort you.

Mona Thank you, Janet. Put them down over there.

Janet I'm doing it.

Mona I'll answer later.

Janet has put the flowers down and gives Mona the card. Janet goes out.

I was in the theatre, remember? I don't want to play the distressed widow. It would be in bad taste. Don't get me wrong, Ray was a friend. My best friend. And I was very fond of him. I nearly called you on Thursday when I got home from the funeral. I wanted to. This was always a big apartment, but that afternoon it seemed ten times bigger. I walked round, touched all the ornaments, the furniture, to make sure they were real. I poured myself a drink, then another.

Donald You were drunk?

Mona Surely you noticed when you called that night?

Donald I was too excited to notice.

Mona I knew that Ingrid would be watching you.

Donald How did you know that?

Mona Because she always is. Do you understand her?

Donald Ingrid?

Mona What's underneath?

Donald All I know: I lived seventeen years without asking that question.

Mona And now?

Donald Lately I've asked myself nothing else.

He is quiet.

I've got so used to it.

Mona Do you never question it?

Donald Not till now. She's like my consciousness. Every breath. She knows every thought, perhaps before I've had it. But she never lets on. She never gives the slightest indication –

Mona Of what?

Donald That she knows. That she knows what I'm thinking.

Mona She knows about us.

There is a silence. Mona shrugs slightly.

Donald She knows?

Mona Why do you think she put the mattresses like that?

Donald You think –

Mona So close together? Inches apart. Didn't you notice? Didn't you think it was odd? At the time?

Donald Maybe she didn't want to seem jealous.

Mona I don't think so.

Donald What then?

Mona Obvious. To test you. I knew what she was doing. She wanted to tempt you. To excite your imagination.

She looks, not yielding.

She kept leaving the room. What was that about?
Leaving us alone. Going shopping. The fridge was full,
you must have realised.

Donald No.

Mona She knew what I wanted.

Donald What did you want exactly?

Mona I wanted your arms around me. I needed comfort.
Face it, she stood aside. Deliberately.

Donald gets up to re-fill the glasses.

I've upset you.

Donald Not at all.

Mona It bothers you.

Donald No.

Mona You still love her, don't you?

Donald No.

Mona But you did? You did love her?

Donald I'm not sure.

Mona Deeply?

Donald speaks clearly, quiet.

Donald I'm beginning to feel I've become like a scientific
experiment. It's like being a microbe under a microscope.

Mona Is that how it feels?

Donald I remember, I married her because she was
tolerant. I thought what's so wonderful about Ingrid is
she never judges. But why was I looking for tolerance?
I hadn't done anything wrong.

There's a moment, then Mona gets up and moves to him.

Mona I want to kiss you.

They kiss again, this time their cheeks together, as though he's comforting her. Then she breaks away.

I need to dress before lunch.

She goes into the bedroom, but she doesn't close the door, leaving it wide open, so she can go on talking. He sits on the sofa, and watches as she sits at the dressing table and brushes her hair. After a few moments, she stops and smiles at him.

You make me laugh.

Donald Why?

Mona You look as if it's the first time you ever watched a woman change.

Donald It may well be.

Mona What about Ingrid? Surely you've watched her getting dressed?

Donald It's not the same thing.

Mona gets up and takes off her house-coat, unself-conscious. Seen through the doorway, the image of her is reminiscent of when Donald saw Ray making love to Patricia. Naked, she moves away out of sight. At once Janet appears with a tray of food which she puts down on a side table. As she turns to go out, Mona passes the doorway naked again, but Janet is unfazed and continues away down the corridor. Mona, out of sight now, is heard from the bedroom.

Mona I thought it easier to have lunch here. Do you mind?

Donald Why would I mind?

Mona I imagined you might want to take me out.

57

Donald You mean, to show you off?

Mona I didn't say that.

Janet returns with an ice bucket and a bottle of white wine.

Donald I'm happier here.

Mona Ray knew a lot about wine. I've picked out something he recommended.

Janet is laying a small table in the middle of the room as Mona reappears at the door. She's in a dress of fine black wool, with a silver belt.

Am I all right? Not overdressed?

Donald You look perfect, Mona.

Mona is sipping her wine. Janet is preparing the buffet and the napkins and cloth. There is lobster and foie gras.

I've never seen you drunk.

Donald You're wrong. I got drunk at the Ashbridges'. Didn't you notice?

Mona Perhaps now you say it. I was thinking –

Donald When?

Mona Another time.

Donald When?

Mona Later. When you'd been out to look for Ray. When you came back. You were strange.

Donald looks to her warningly in front of Janet, not wanting to speak. But Janet now goes out. They're alone.

Donald I wasn't drunk.

Mona So tell me.

Donald If the truth doesn't frighten you.

He gets up, knowing he's about to cross a line.

When I went out to look for him, I didn't look. I didn't search.

Mona What did you do?

Donald I went out, the storm was raging. It was pitch black. The wind, the snow were blowing right into my eyes. So I went into the barn, I sat on a bench and I started to smoke.

Mona You were gone –

Donald Two hours. More.

Mona You were in the barn all the time?

Donald I smoked at least ten. Maybe a dozen. Then I came back.

Mona is completely still. She is shaken, but she is not angry. She reaches out a hand. Donald takes it.

Mona Thank you.

Donald For what?

Mona For telling me. I knew something had happened. I thought perhaps you'd had a fight –

Donald With Ray?

Mona Some sort of quarrel.

Donald Of course not. Why would I fight with Ray?

Mona For the obvious reason.

She shrugs slightly.

Because I could see how upset you were.

Donald When?

Mona When do you think? At the party, of course.
You'd been to the bathroom. He was in there, wasn't he?

Donald nods.

With that ridiculous woman?

Donald Patricia.

Mona Yes. Patricia.

Donald The third Mrs Ashbridge.

Mona You saw them?

Donald How did you know?

Mona Because I saw them too. Heading off together.
And I could see that didn't make you happy. You were
jealous, weren't you?

Donald Not because of her.

Mona No. Because of me.

She is crumbling a bread roll in her hand.

Donald I don't know how to describe it. Except to say it
was everything. My whole life. I opened the bathroom
door and somehow – there's a history you don't know. At
Yale. I was top of the year. The brightest student they had.

Mona Ray said you were brilliant.

Donald Whatever. I was going places. And when Ray
went off to Manhattan, I thought, he'll fail. How wrong
can you be? Today I live precisely thirty miles from my
father. Why? Because I was frightened.

Mona Frightened of what?

Donald The world. I wanted some sort of – I don't know – protection? Is that the word? I married Ingrid. More protection. I was frightened and Ray wasn't.

Mona Drink.

He takes a sip of wine.

Donald You can guess the rest.

Mona I can now, yes.

Donald Somehow – I opened the bathroom door –

Mona I understand –

Donald Ray had whatever he wanted. There it was. Whatever came to hand. Even when he didn't want it. Not just you, it wasn't just you – his whole life was easy – any woman, at any time –

Mona smiles.

I'm disappointing you, I'm sure.

Mona Not at all.

Donald This is not who you wanted me to be. It's as if I've lived my whole life with the handbrake on.

Mona reaches out for his hand and grips it tighter.

Mona It takes tremendous courage.

Donald Courage?

Mona To tell me these things. And not to care what I think.

Donald I do care what you think.

Mona You hated Ray, didn't you?

Donald No. Only that night. Seeing him with that woman.

Mona Is that why you drove off the road? Because you were angry?

Donald No. No, I promise you, that was the snow.

He stops, intense now.

Mona But when we got home, then what happened?

Donald I knew I had to go out and look for Ray. When I went out searching, I reached the barn and I thought 'Why don't I sit for a few moments before I go any further?' But a few moments became a couple of hours. I went in as one man, and I came out as another.

Mona How is that possible?

Donald Oh it's very possible, I promise you.

Mona How?

Donald It was as though I was lucid. I could see.

Mona See what?

Donald I'd always been in control. Or so I thought. But I wasn't. I never had been. I thought I despised Manhattan. Oh, the stupid life of the city and the stupid people who take it seriously. The ones who care about whether they get into restaurants or not, and then whether they have the right table, the right seat. Tickets for the right show. Whether the right people say hello to them. I thought I'd rejected that life. But in the barn I realised I hadn't rejected it. It had rejected me.

Mona Donald . . .

Donald Truly. I went into a kind of trance. The wind was blowing so hard I thought the roof would blow off. And the door was off its hinges, and it was banging. Banging. I knew I'd fooled myself. All my life. When Ray disappeared, oh, at once, I was sent to look for him. We all agreed it was urgent. When I disappeared, nobody cared.

He shrugs, as if that sums things up.

At the party I'd been standing beside Ashbridge when he met Ray, and to Ray of course he was effusive. But when he looked at me, it wasn't contempt. It was barely even indifference. Because to people like Harold I don't exist. When he first arrived in town, Harold said to me, 'I must talk to you one of these days. About business.' But he forgot. He never talked to me. Of course not. Why would he? I didn't mind. I'd never minded. Because I thought he was an idiot. A rich idiot.

He shakes his head.

Then Ray took Harold's wife into the bathroom. As if it were nothing, as if it were just what you do. You take a woman into the bathroom and fuck her. And, for me, everything began to hurt. For the first time. All the slights that had meant nothing, now they did mean something. They meant I'd lost, lost in life, and lost profoundly. So later I admit, I found myself thinking 'I'm not going to look for Ray. Why should I? It's pointless anyway. I'm never going to find him. He's dead. The storm is blowing and he's dead.' I thought, 'I can fool myself that I'm going to find him, like I've fooled myself about everything all my life. Ingrid wants me to look, so I'll *say* I looked. But I won't. I'll just sit here. It's easier.' And somehow – can't say why – it was comforting to sit in the snow and know that I'd been wrong. Wrong about everything. And one of the things was – I'd always thought of Ray as my best friend. And now I was thinking, 'If he's your best friend why are you letting him die?'

He looks at Mona and nods slightly.

Oh, I didn't murder him. No. But it was as if I did.

Mona is looking him straight in the eye across the table.

I've always been frightened my heart will stop. Since I was a child, I've had that fear. One moment it'll be beating and then it won't. It'll just stop. If I hadn't been worried about my heart, perhaps I'd have stayed in the barn all night.

Mona And if he had been there – if you could – would you have saved him?

Donald I don't know. I've asked myself that. I really don't know.

He's slightly hoarse. He takes another drink.

Mona I could tell something was peculiar when you came back. Something jarred. Ingrid sensed it too.

Donald I'm sure. Because next day she went to the barn – she found my cigarette butts –

Mona She found your cigarettes?

Donald Yes.

Mona She's something, isn't she?

Donald Brought them back to the house.

Mona She protected you?

Donald In case Olsen found them.

Mona But did she think –

Donald What?

Mona Does she think – you know what I'm saying –

Donald Does she think I pushed Ray over a rock? I don't know. These past few days, she's certainly been looking at me as if – as if I've changed.

Mona You have changed.

They both smile slightly.

Donald Yesterday we went to see the girls. And I was

happy to see them. I don't know what else is real to me, but the girls are real. I love them.

Mona I'm sure.

Donald I love them very much. And I like to think I've been a good father.

Mona I'm sure you have.

Donald But yesterday I felt I was acting. I've been acting since that night.

He looks at her a moment.

Does that sound stupid?

Mona Don't you get tired of your character? Ray did. I've got a feeling I may be a bit tired of mine.

Donald I can't see why.

Mona Oh –

Donald I can't see anything wrong with you at all.

Mona There's plenty wrong. I'd like to change.

Donald Then what's stopping you?

Mona I don't think I can do it alone.

Donald looks at her, the decisive moment reached. Then he looks down.

Donald I'm not sure what you're asking. I can't leave Ingrid if that's what you mean.

Mona wipes some crumbs from her dress, and then gets up.

Mona Thank you, Donald.

Donald Not now.

Mona Look, I don't –

Donald Not straight away –

Mona It's all right.

Donald Just to be clear. After so many years. Please. Imagine. When we've only just – it's not like –

Mona Don't say any more.

She gets up, slightly panicky.

Do you want coffee?

Donald Yes, please.

Mona (*raising her voice*) Janet!

Janet appears at once.

We both want coffee. Thank you.

Janet goes.

Shall we talk business?

Donald Why, yes.

There's no bitterness in her voice, and in fact Donald is already up getting his briefcase.

First of all, do you know how you stand?

Mona No, I don't.

Donald No inkling?

Mona Ray never talked about money.

Donald is getting out some papers.

Donald I went to see his partners.

Mona When?

Donald This morning. First thing.

Mona Were they friendly to you?

66

Donald Polite, anyway. Wondering, I'm sure, why I'd been chosen. They gave me a copy of the partnership agreement. The Millers are deleting his name from the plate.

Mona Already?

Donald I looked at the papers on the way here.

He holds up the relevant paper.

I've also looked at your life insurance.

Mona Oh yes, I'd forgotten about that.

Donald Did you know it was worth two hundred thousand dollars?

Mona No. I didn't.

Donald And the partnership agreement means another five. That's what the Millers are offering to buy Ray out. You're a rich woman.

Mona Seven hundred thousand?

Donald Exactly.

Mona As much as that?

Donald Yes.

Mona It's amazing. It's going to take a moment to sink in.

She seems dazed rather than pleased.

Donald I think perhaps I should stay at a hotel tonight, get all your business sorted out.

Mona Does it have to be a hotel? You could stay here. Well?

Donald I was thinking of Janet.

Mona Do you think she doesn't know already? Lunch?

They smile and sit down for lunch opposite each other.

Donald I'll call Ingrid. I'll tell her I'm at the Algonquin.

Mona What if she calls you back?

Donald Do you think she doesn't know too?

FOURTEEN

Darkness. The sound of a phone conversation.

Donald (*voice*) Ingrid, it's Donald.

Ingrid (*voice*) Donald.

Donald (*voice*) Well, you were right.

Ingrid (*voice*) I thought I might be.

Donald (*voice*) I shan't make it home tonight.

Ingrid (*voice*) I expected that.

Donald (*voice*) The Millers have given me a lot of paperwork, so Mona and I will need to go see them tomorrow.

Ingrid (*voice*) That's great. I knew you'd be able to help her.

Donald (*voice*) Yes. I think I can.

Ingrid (*voice*) Are you at the Algonquin?

Donald (*voice*) Not yet. I will be.

Ingrid (*voice*) Good. Give my love to Mona.

Donald (*voice*) I'll pass that on.

Ingrid (*voice*) Don't forget. 'Bye, Donald.

Donald (*voice*) 'Bye.

Part Three: Ingrid

FIFTEEN

The garden at Yellow Rock Farm. There is a blaze of daffodils growing wild. Ingrid approaches with a trug. She looks at the flowers thoughtfully, then after a few moments she reaches down and, with secateurs, she neatly cuts them, with surgical precision. She lays them in the trug and moves on.

SIXTEEN

The living room at Yellow Rock Farm. The place is transformed by the change of light. Sunshine streaming in the windows, the snow long gone. Donald is reading the Torrington Citizen *as Ingrid comes in at the back, carrying the trug, loaded with daffodils.*

Ingrid Daffodils.

Donald Thank goodness.

Ingrid What a winter.

Donald Yes.

Ingrid Over at last.

She goes to get a vase, but continues talking.

I sometimes wonder whether they're a domestic flower. Whether they should be cut at all.

Donald Hmm.

Ingrid My mother always said there was something sad about cut flowers. But daffodils especially.

Donald I don't think so. They cheer the place up.

Ingrid returns with a vase, and starts filling it with flowers, cutting their stalks evenly with scissors.

Ingrid You're enjoying Manhattan? The trips you've been taking?

Donald It's not about enjoyment. It's about work.

Ingrid Mona must be grateful.

Donald She is.

Ingrid You've been so often.

Donald It turned out to be more complicated than it looked.

Ingrid I'm sure you're dealing with it.

Donald If you like you're welcome to come with me.

Ingrid You're going again?

Donald No choice.

Ingrid just looks at him.

Why don't you?

Ingrid You know perfectly well.

Donald Tell me.

Ingrid I've never felt comfortable in the city. To be honest, I've never needed it.

Donald I don't know how you can say that.

Ingrid All that agitation. It's a substitute, isn't it?

Donald Substitute for what?

Ingrid For life.

Donald It is life.

Ingrid Is it?

Donald Just with more intensity.

Ingrid I'm happier here.

Donald I think charity would grind to a halt altogether in Lakeville if you weren't around.

Ingrid starts arranging the vase.

Ingrid My father had an apartment on Park Avenue, remember? He never used it. It didn't interest him.

Donald I liked your father. I remember him saying, 'I don't know why I'm the surgeon in the family. It should be Ingrid. She's more accurate.'

Ingrid That's Daddy.

She smiles, thrilled at the remark.

Big apartment it was. You never saw it?

Donald No. He'd sold it by then.

Ingrid I was going to live there when I went to study art. That was the idea. I thought I was going to paint. But then I met you.

She is not looking at him.

Donald And do you remember what you saw in me?

Ingrid When?

Donald At the beginning?

Ingrid Why are you asking?

Donald Ingrid.

Ingrid You don't really want me to say?

Donald Yes, I do.

Ingrid What did I see at the beginning? Same thing I see in you now.

Donald And what is that?

She looks at him a moment, then shrugs.

Ingrid I saw a man I could live with.

There's a moment's silence.

You asked. I'm telling you.

Donald Just that? Nothing more?

Ingrid In my book, that's quite something.

Donald What are you saying? You mean you chose me?

Ingrid I think I did.

Donald Did I have anything to do with it?

Ingrid Do you want the honest answer?

Donald Yes.

Ingrid Not much.

Ingrid smiles.

You had a pleasing modesty. I liked that. Something about the sports jacket you were wearing.

Donald The jacket?

Ingrid As if you didn't care what people thought of you.

Donald You chose me because I was badly dressed?

Ingrid Not at all. Because you were carelessly dressed. It's different. It was a good sign. You weren't calculating.

Donald And when you got to know me better?

Ingrid I knew who you were the moment I met you.

Donald That doesn't make me sound very interesting.

Ingrid I mean it as a compliment. I've always been chaos-averse. Nothing you've done has ever surprised me.

She just looks. Donald is quietly angry.

Donald I took the bench out.

Ingrid Yes.

Donald Did you notice?

Ingrid I saw you'd done that.

Donald From the barn. I always take it out. Every spring. When the weather gets warm.

He throws a glance towards her, but she is working on the flowers, not reacting.

I've been meaning to ask you. About the cigarette butts. Why did you pick them up? Why did you do that?

Ingrid I thought they looked untidy down there.

Donald Untidy?

Ingrid Yes.

Donald Was that the only reason?

Ingrid They were yours, weren't they?

Donald You know they were.

Ingrid I thought they must have been.

Donald Does anything ever escape you?

Ingrid I didn't want Lieutenant Olsen to be distracted. He might have been misled. That's why I picked them up.

Donald puts down the paper angrily and goes across to get a scotch.

Donald I'm going to have a drink. Do you want one?

Ingrid doesn't answer.

Just saying, but I'm going to have to go back to New York.

Ingrid Yes you said.

Donald I've sorted out Mona's finances, but now it's her apartment.

Ingrid What about it?

Donald She wants to downsize.

Ingrid Does that make things difficult?

Donald It's a question of probate. It's complicated.

Ingrid carries on with the flowers.

Ingrid You haven't forgotten Easter? The girls.

Donald I'll be back by Easter.

Ingrid We promised them we'd go hiking, now the weather's warmer.

Donald Good.

Ingrid It's the girls I worry about. I want them to grow up strong and true. Like oaks. I want nothing for myself, but for Cecilia and Mildred I want everything. As far as I'm concerned, they can't have enough. I'm not talking about money. I'm talking about a certain quality to things. Call it openness. Call it honesty.

There is a silence.

Yes, Donald. I love this part of the world. The way of life. Everything's slipping away. And I like the idea of a place which still has value. Where I was born.

They are staring at each other now.

74

Donald About the cigarette butts.

Ingrid What?

Donald You picked them up, you said.

Ingrid Well so I did.

Donald You brought them in.

Ingrid That's right.

Donald And you intended to throw them away? Funny how you didn't.

Ingrid I forgot.

Donald Not like you.

Ingrid I was going to.

Donald But?

Ingrid But I never got round to it.

Donald You wanted me to find them, didn't you? You wanted me to know who'd saved me.

For the first time, Donald raises his voice.

'Call it openness! Call it honesty!'

Ingrid Sometimes I've noticed there's an unkindness in you, Donald. It's part of your make-up. But I'll tell you something about that. If you really love someone, you love everything about them. You love them for their faults as well.

Donald Meaning?

Ingrid And because of that, you get to a point where you can't be hurt. However hard the other person is trying, you simply can't be hurt. Regardless.

Donald Regardless?

Ingrid Yes.

Donald Not in code, Ingrid. Tell me. Specifically.

But Ingrid just smiles.

What do you think happened that night?

Ingrid I don't know.

Donald But you want to know?

Ingrid If I wanted to know then I'd ask.

Donald You prefer not to know because you prefer to think the worst.

Ingrid Is there a worst?

Donald You think I was derelict? You think Ray died and it's my fault?

Ingrid I've never said that.

Donald No, but you quite like that, don't you? It suits you, doesn't it? Keeping me where I belong. Always in the wrong.

Ingrid looks at him, nodding.

Ingrid You're like many men. You live in your own idea of life. It's the only place you're happy. You don't live in life itself. It doesn't bother me. I've dealt with it. So have the girls. We always will.

Donald Because you think no one else will take me? No one else wants me?

Ingrid Other people want you, I'm sure. You're a catch. But none of them will live with you.

There is a silence. Ingrid holds up the vase.

How are the flowers?

Donald Great.

SEVENTEEN

Torrington, Connecticut. An intercom conversation in the dark.

Donald (*voice*) Hello. Hello.

Dodd (*voice*) Where are you?

Donald (*voice*) Where do you think, for goodness' sake? I'm outside. It seems to be locked.

Dodd (*voice*) It is locked.

Donald (*voice*) What I'm asking: can you open it?

Dodd (*voice*) Are you in a car?

Donald (*voice*) I am. I put it in the marked space.

There is a slight silence.

Well, are you going to let me in?

EIGHTEEN

The offices of the Citizen, *Torrington. Mr Dodd is leading Donald into the deserted room, which is archaic in feel: a small traditional pre-war local newspaper. Mr Dodd is in his seventies, tall, scrawny, from another age.*

Dodd It's Saturday. We're not open.

Donald Well, it was you who asked to see me, if you remember.

Dodd Are you going somewhere?

Donald And then I have to fight to get in.

Dodd You're in now.

Donald I have no reason to be in Torrington except to come by. It's been a long time.

Dodd You've had a lot going on. I understand. You're in good health?

He has sat down in the editor's chair, and picked up proofs without thinking. Donald nods.

Donald You?

Dodd Oh – How old are you?

Donald Forty-five.

Dodd You've passed the halfway mark.

Donald Some time ago.

Dodd smiles to himself, as if satisfied.

I'm glad we're back in touch.

Dodd Were we ever out?

Donald I was surprised when you didn't call.

Dodd When?

Donald When you ran the story.

Dodd Oh. Had no need to.

Donald You reported it, but you didn't call to talk to us.

Dodd Talk to you about what?

Donald I lost my best friend.

Dodd I knew that.

Donald Perhaps we could have given you some facts.

Dodd I had the facts.

Donald Not all of them.

Dodd If you say so.

Donald Well?

Dodd I didn't want to look too closely because I wasn't sure what I might find.

Donald Then at least to see if we were all right.

Dodd It's your life.

Donald And what exactly do you mean by that, Dad?

Dodd is stubborn, silent.

Dodd Have you come across the county to pick a fight with me?

Donald No, I haven't. It's just when you say 'It's your life' I'm pretty sure what you're getting at.

Dodd (*shrugs*) It's your life.

Donald You alluding to Mona?

Dodd I didn't know she was called Mona.

Donald Then who told you I had a girlfriend?

Dodd Very few people who don't tell me. Everyone knows. Everyone's known for months.

Donald Have they?

Dodd All the trips you make to the city.

Donald They're waiting at Millerton Station, are they? Checking me out? Checking me in?

Dodd They say she's the widow of your friend Ray.

Donald They're right.

Dodd And he died in a blizzard at your place. I have the right man, don't I?

Donald blushes, unable to answer.

Dodd I own a newspaper. I'm at the centre of the community.

Donald What community? There is no community. A few people pleased with themselves because in 1954 they read a book. And in 1955 they went to the opera. And that makes them better than all the peasants who live to the west.

Dodd If you don't like it here, you know what to do.

Donald I've lived here all my life.

Dodd Then maybe it's time to think about moving on.

Donald And when exactly did you ever move on? At least I don't live in a museum.

Dodd is furious, and his voice is more intense.

Dodd A man died. It's not me who puts two and two together.

Donald Then who is it?

Dodd The entire adult population of Canaan, Lakeville and Torrington.

Donald What business is it of theirs?

Dodd That's the very question, same question I put when people ask me. As they do.

Donald What else do they ask?

Dodd 'Are you going to divorce? Are you going to live in New York?'

Donald I'll tell you.

Dodd I didn't ask you, so I don't need the answer.

He lights his pipe and sits back.

Donald Dad, I'm beginning to think this visit may be a mistake.

Dodd I know why you're here. You're here because Ingrid came by.

Donald Ingrid?

Dodd Yes.

Donald Ingrid came here? She never told me.

Dodd Doesn't mean it didn't happen.

Donald When?

Dodd When you were away.

Donald What did she want?

Dodd And now suddenly you're interested. Never cared about people unless you could get something from them.

Donald Tell me: did she talk about Mona?

Dodd And that's it. That's what you want to know.

Donald Information, Dad, that's your trade. Not withholding it.

Dodd looks at him with contempt.

Dodd I remember the first day you brought Ingrid here. She was standing where you're standing. Came from Litchfield. Even owned a horse. Your mother and I thought you were making a mistake. We were wrong. You can be mistaken about people, you see. Ingrid wouldn't dream of talking about whatever your woman's called. She wouldn't stoop to it. Not with her own father-in-law. She turned out one of the best people I ever knew.

Donald You mean, not a disappointment, like me?

Dodd I didn't say that.

Donald Ever since Stuart died. If you want to feel adequate in life, never have an older brother who dies in the war.

Dodd I won't hear a word against Stuart.

Donald No, exactly.

Dodd is not yielding an inch.

And your idea of goodness, Dad, it's keeping quiet, is it? Is that what goodness is? Saying nothing? Putting up with things? Does that make you a good man?

Dodd I've never claimed to be good.

Donald Editing the *Citizen* for forty years?

Dodd Forty-six.

Donald The same newspaper. The same opinions. Do you think anyone reads your pathetic newspaper any more?

Dodd I'm getting near the end, I know that.

Donald 'This vulgar development threatens the essential character of Torrington.' 'The community has expressed its view and now it's the responsibility of its leaders to act.' Please! Do you think anyone gives a damn? It's over! Do you think that stuff makes sense any more? Why am I trapped? I'm trapped because my father was trapped. And my girls will be trapped after me.

Dodd I can see your affair is bringing out the worst in you.

Donald has raised his voice.

Donald It's not an affair.

Dodd So you say.

Donald Mona's everything I never had for forty-five years.

Dodd Your mother would not have been happy.

Donald My mother was never happy. Least of all with me.

Dodd Well then.

He shakes his head.

Ingrid didn't talk to me. No. She sat in the chair you're sitting in now and she said not a word. Not a word for you. Not a word against. She didn't need to. She and I know.

Donald Know what?

Dodd Who you are.

Donald is furious.

Donald I've been a good husband. And most of all, I've been a good father.

Dodd You sound as if you want a reward. Life isn't like that. Do it for its own sake or not at all.

Donald I came here to make contact. That's why I came.

Dodd Contact your wife. She didn't say anything, but I knew: that's why. Ingrid's a woman with standards, and those standards still mean something, whatever you say. Because in this life, I can tell you one thing, there aren't any others.

Donald That's what you believe.

He turns to go. His father does not move. Donald turns back at the door.

Just so you know: it's taken me a whole lifetime but perhaps I'm beginning at last to understand myself.

Dodd That's a foolish thing for anyone to say.

Donald Is it? Why?

Dodd Because it's never true.

Donald In my case, I think it is. And I'm finally ready to do something about it.

Dodd If that means you're going to go off and live with that woman, then maybe that's the best thing for you.

Donald Yes. Maybe it is. It's taken me a long time to reach this point, but whatever happens, I'm not backing down.

Dodd Fine.

They look at each other for a moment.

Donald Dad, I don't need to live among people who disapprove of me.

Dodd In that case, you may end up decidedly short of company.

NINETEEN

A phone conversation, in the dark.

Donald (*voice*) Mona, you're there.

Mona (*voice*) Yes.

Donald (*voice*) I called earlier.

Mona (*voice*) I was away for a few days on Long Island. I told you I was going.

Donald (*voice*) But you're back?

Mona (*voice*) You're going to be surprised. I swam, I got a tan, I played tennis. Amazing how quickly my game came back.

Donald (*voice*) Maybe I could come by tomorrow?

Mona (*voice*) Remind me what day that is.

Donald (*voice*) Tomorrow? Wednesday.

Mona (*voice*) Let's do it then.

TWENTY

Sutton Place. It's late in the day, darker than before. It's also emptier, some of the furniture's gone. Mona is going to the door in a light emerald-green suit. She opens it. Donald stands a moment.

Mona You're taken aback.

Donald No. No, just not quite what I was expecting.

Mona I'm sorry.

Donald smiles. She kisses him for a few moments.

Donald You're dressed.

Mona Are you disappointed?

Donald looks round.

Yes, I've sold some furniture since you last came.

Donald It seems empty.

Mona I won't be here much longer.

Donald Do you want me to take you to dinner?

Mona Later. First I want to talk. Do you mind?

Donald Janet not around?

Mona I gave her the day off. So we could be alone.

Donald How was Long Island? You went riding?

Mona Got thrown off a couple of times but I picked myself up. There were a lot of people out there.

Donald A lot?

Mona At one point, twenty.

Donald Wow.

Mona has sat down and is looking at him.

Mona We're old friends, you and I, aren't we? You're the best friend I ever had.

Donald has sat too. He doesn't reply.

You know John Falk?

Donald I don't think I do.

Mona Watch the best serials on CBS. He's a producer. His name's a hallmark of quality. His work is hugely influential. I've known him – since my father was alive. He's a year older than me. He's been divorced for three years. One child. A girl.

Again, nothing.

We've decided to get married.

Donald can't think of anything to say.

Forgive me.

Donald What for?

Mona For hurting you.

Donald A little.

Mona I've been meaning to talk to you about him for some time. I didn't know what was best. I was thinking of getting the two of you together, so I could take your advice. I wanted you to meet him and tell me what you thought of him.

Donald But you didn't.

Mona I was going to.

Donald When is it going to happen?

Mona It's some way off.

Donald Weeks? Months?

Mona Legal stuff. Again. And also, finding an apartment because Monique's going to live with us. He has custody and he's the most wonderful father. He adores his kid. I thought someone who really loves his child like that –

Donald says nothing.

I'm hoping you and I can still be friends.

Donald After you marry?

Mona That's why I told John about you.

Donald You told him?

Mona Yes.

Donald Did you tell him everything?

Mona Donald, he hardly thinks I'm a virgin.

She has said it carelessly, in a tone which shocks Donald.

You didn't guess? Sometimes, those lunches we had together, those dinners, they got a little awkward, didn't they?

Donald Did they?

Mona Like we didn't know what to say to one another. I was always happy with you. But even so.

Donald makes no response.

Donald I'd like to ask one question.

Mona Anything.

Donald The first day I came. I don't know if you remember –

Mona I remember clearly.

Donald Just after you and I – when we came out of the bedroom for the first time, there were some flowers –

Mona Yes.

Donald Janet carried them across to you.

Mona Yes.

Donald Gave you a card. From a family friend.

Mona That was John.

Donald Even then.

Donald can find nothing more to say.

Mona I told him we were going to have this conversation.

Donald Today?

Mona Yes.

Donald He knows we're meeting?

Mona Yes.

Donald Right now?

Mona I felt I owed him that.

Donald Is he waiting for you to call? To say everything's gone fine?

Mona ignores this.

Mona Donald, I hope you'll come and see us.

Donald I know Mona. I don't know Mrs Falk.

He looks away, on the point of tears.

Mona And what I'm most happy about, I can act again.

Donald Act?

Mona Yes. That *is* what I do for a living. John's always wanted me to go back to it. He's got a good part for me. In a series. I mostly did stage, but now I feel ready to do television. It's a different technique, but I'd like a go at it. I only didn't act while I was with Ray.

Donald nods, thinking about it.

Donald Do you think about him?

Mona Who?

Donald Ray.

Mona Often. We were married for six years.

Donald You told me he thought about killing himself. He was lucky. He didn't have to jump. He didn't have to cut his throat. What a stroke of luck!

Mona is shocked, but level.

Mona I'm sorry, Donald, I know it's hard. But it was you who said it wouldn't work.

Donald Did I say that?

Mona You weren't in love.

Donald I wasn't. I am now.

Mona Oh men! You're all so competitive.

She gets up.

I'm going to make you a scotch.

Donald Thank you.

Mona The way you like it.

Donald watches her move across.

I'm going to remember this apartment. Every detail of it. And everything that happened between us in these rooms.

For the rest of my life. This is where it all happened.

Donald does not react.

Donald When are you due to call him?

Mona comes across to him with the scotch.

Mona Courage, Donald.

Donald To you, Mona.

Mona To you.

They both drink. Then Mona puts her glass down and returns to give Donald a long kiss.

Thank you, Donald. I've loved the time that we've had together.

Donald Aren't you going to ask me what I'm going to do?

Mona smiles.

Mona But I know what you'll do. You'll go back to Ingrid.

TWENTY-ONE

Mona takes Donald to the door. Overlapping with this, Ingrid sits down to play patience at a small green-felt table. Mona says goodbye to Donald who does not reply. Donald goes. Mona, relieved, walks back into the room. For a moment the two women are on separate parts of the stage, then Mona walks off down the corridor. Ingrid, unperturbed, continues playing as the stage image changes around her.

The living room of Yellow Rock Farm. Donald is in a chair reading the paper at the other side of the room.

Ingrid Do you realise what you're doing?

Donald No. No I don't.

Ingrid You hadn't noticed? You must have noticed.

Ingrid laughs. Donald has no idea what she's asking.

It's funny. Are you really reading that paper?

Donald Yes.

Ingrid Really? Those glasses.

Donald takes off the glasses he's wearing.

Donald I hadn't noticed. But they're better than mine.

He holds them out to her as Ingrid gathers up her cards.

Here.

Ingrid I'm out. You're not having a whisky?

Donald I'm not.

Ingrid You don't seem to drink any more.

Donald I've lost interest. Also: I'm worried about the pills. Mixing drink and pills. I've been sleeping badly.

Ingrid I hear you. Every night.

Donald I know you do. I try to be quiet. I keep as quiet as I can.

The doorbell rings, absurdly loud.

Who's that?

Ingrid Well, I should imagine it's Dr Warren.

Donald Dr Warren? What's he doing here?

Ingrid Surely you remember?

Donald No.

He goes to the door and opens it. Dr Warren has a dossier under his arm.

Dr Warren Ah good, Donald, excellent.

Ingrid Dr Warren.

Dr Warren Ingrid.

Ingrid Donald seems to have forgotten.

Donald Tell me what I've forgotten.

Dr Warren My taxes. We arranged that I'd come by and you'd look at my taxes.

Donald Is that right?

Dr Warren We made a plan.

Ingrid If you two are going to talk, then I'm going to bed. Donald, you'll find me when you come up. You won't forget to turn everything out?

Donald I won't forget.

Ingrid Thank you. Excuse me, Doctor. Goodnight.

She goes out. Warren holds out the dossier.

Dr Warren Everything you need is in here.

Donald Do you think I believe you? Do you think I believe you for one minute?

Dr Warren I'm sorry?

Donald Are you observing me? How do you judge me? Did she call you?

Dr Warren Who?

Donald Ingrid.

Dr Warren My dear Donald – I'm here on business.

Donald Are you?

Dr Warren Yes. Look. My tax affairs.

Donald ignores the folder.

Donald You've spoken to her, haven't you? When? Since her victory?

Dr Warren I don't know what her victory is.

Donald waits. Warren is extremely uncomfortable.

Donald Did she tell you what happened? She knows, doesn't she? Oh, she doesn't say so, anything rather than let on, she'd die rather than say anything to me, she never admits anything to me, but she knows. She's got what she wants. She wins. End of story. Didn't she say?

Dr Warren Donald, I'm a professional. The first rule: I respect confidence. At all times.

Donald I take that as a yes.

Dr Warren Take it any way you want.

Donald She knows.

Dr Warren Knows what?

Donald And so do you.

He waits, but Warren can't answer.

What do you want me to say? I'm beaten? I surrender?

Dr Warren Surrender what?

Donald has raised his voice, angry now.

Donald Are there any tests you can give me? Is there a pill? Can you open your bag and give me a pill? Do I seem odd to you because I've started telling people the truth? Have you seen enough? Can you go back to Ingrid tomorrow and say, 'Yes, he's angry but, don't worry, he'll be fine'? After all, you're Ingrid's friend much more than mine. Everyone is.

Dr Warren I don't know why but you seem angry with me.

Donald No. Not you. I'm not angry with anyone. Not even Ingrid. I'm angry with myself. So long ago, I took a wrong path. So long ago. A lifetime. Everyone else knows their part. I don't know mine.

Warren cannot think of anything to say.

I think about her hand.

Dr Warren Her hand?

Donald Mona's hand. Lying beside me on the mattress. And why I didn't dare take it. I wanted to. I wanted to take it. If I'd taken it, what would have happened then?

Warren looks, then gets up.

I'm going to come back another time.

Donald When I'm back to normal?

Warren stops at the door.

Dr Warren Whatever you do, please look after your wife. She's very loved in the community.

Warren goes out. Donald stands a moment, as if listening.

TWENTY-TWO

The bedroom at Yellow Rock Farm. It's the middle of the night. Donald and Ingrid are lying side by side. He is awake, she seems to be asleep. He reaches into the drawer in a table beside the bed and takes a pill. Then he takes another. Then another. He lies a moment, then he gets out of bed and goes to the bathroom. He turns the light on, so a shaft falls into the bedroom. Ingrid wakes and sits up. She waits a few moments.

Ingrid Donald.

No reply.

Donald. Aren't you feeling well?

She waits, sitting up. After some moments, Donald comes back and opens the bedside drawer again. He takes out a revolver, and turns the barrel towards her. She looks at him, steady, saying nothing. He shoots her in the chest, but she remains still. Then he shoots at both her eyes. Her body barely moves but blood runs from her eyes. He throws the gun down on the bed. He stands a moment, then he goes to the bedside telephone. He dials. The stage darkens. The sound of a telephone conversation.

Olsen (*voice*) Olsen.

Donald Lieutenant Olsen?

Olsen (*voice*) Yes.

Donald This is Donald Dodd. I shot her in the eyes.

There is a silence. The stage is still darkening.

Olsen (*voice*) Mr Dodd, are you there? Are you there?

More silence.

I'm coming right over. Don't do anything foolish.

Dark.